How to Start a Pool Service

A Simple Six Step Guide

By Jeffrey M. Schulte

Why a pool business?

A pool service can be a fun and profitable way to make a living while working outside and staying in shape at the same time. You won't find overweight pool service guys or girls. This work can be very physical and if you aren't up to the task of servicing at least ten pools a day then you might want to consider another line of work. But if you feel that you can service at least 50 or more pools per week, then you can be making as much as $50,000 a year. As much as you want to work is as much money that you will make. I have a friend in the business that was servicing 110 accounts a week by himself. You can figure that he will gross nearly $120,000 for the year. He works Saturdays, gets home late, and has back problems, so like any profession, there are drawbacks as well.

When I decided to get into this business, I didn't know much more than the average pool user. I have been a swimmer nearly all of my life and have spent more time in pools than the average person, but really didn't know much of what is involved in the business of servicing pools. This guide will provide a brief introduction into the business that I have been involved in for the last several years. When I started, there was very little information on the pool business and the closest guide I could find cost $250. In this guide, I will try to simplify the process of getting started and give you the benefit of my experience.

This book is not intended to be a complete and comprehensive guide to the pool service business, but is intended to give you an idea of the finances, effort, laws, chemicals, and customer service issues that you will face should you decide to jump in the water, and help you to avoid some of the pitfalls of getting started on your own and having to learn it all the hard way as I did.

Step 1. Education

In the state of Florida where I live and many other states, you need to be certified, especially if you want to service commercial accounts. You need to be at least 18 years old and so there are no pool "boys."

Certification also lends to your credibility as a professional when you are trying to promote yourself and your business.

How?

You will need to take a class or seminar that is approved by your state. An internet search of your state's professional licensing bureau will list the approved vendors offering a certification class. You can even take an on-line class. Don't think the on-line class is easier. It is not easier but it can be more convenient if travel or time is a constraint for you. Classes can be from three days to a week, and the on-line class will require a minimum of 16 hours on-line time, not counting your own required research and assignments.

This class will cost anywhere from $250 for the on-line class to as much as $1000 for a week class. You have to keep in mind that like all education, it gives you a base of knowledge to start with. Real knowledge only comes with combining your classroom knowledge with your real-world experience, so if you can spend a day with a pool service guy you will gain some real-world knowledge and you can pay to go along with him on his route for a few days to see what it's really all about. You might even try this first before you invest in the class to see if it really is for you and if you can see yourself doing it by yourself all day and week long.

The deliverable and end result of your class is a printed Professional Pool Operators or Technician certificate that you can show any potential customers to establish credibility and a level of expertise as a pool professional.

Step 2. Paperwork and Legal Issues.

If you have not been in business for yourself or have ever started a business before, you need to understand some of the basics of getting yourself set-up as a legitimate business.

A. **Legal organization:** Are you going to be a sole proprietor, a corporation, a partnership, or a LLC (Limited Liability Company)? I recommend an LLC as it is usually easy to set up and the paperwork requirements for the state are pretty simple and straight-forward. An LLC allows you to insulate your personal liability from your business, which can come in handy if you should face a lawsuit for some odd reason.

B. **Fictitious Name Filing:** You need to have a business bank account and pick a name for your business. When people pay you for your service, they will make a check out to your "Doing Business As" or DBA. You can usually file on-line for a fictitious name and the cost is minimal. When you open your business bank account they will want to see the official DBA form. Pick a name that is simple, describes what you do, and is memorable. Remember that you

SHOULD have a website for your business and a short name will be easier to use for a web address.

c. **Federal Employer's Identification Number or EIN:** Do yourself a favor and don't try to hide from the IRS. They will catch you sooner or later. Consult your attorney or tax man for the most advantageous business organization for you, but you need to file for an EIN which you can do on-line as well, and any bank or vendor will often ask you for your taxpayer's ID or EIN.

D. **Business License**: You need to check your

locality for the requirements of a business

license. It will differ from town, city, state or

wherever, so you have to make a couple of calls

to your town hall to see what the requirements

are. As long as you don't make a lot of noise,

don't create a traffic problem, and don't attract

a lot of attention to yourself, you can work out

of your home and write off the expenses for

using part of your home for business. As always,

talk to your tax man for specifics.

E. **Business Cards, Signage, and**

Stationery: You can get it all very reasonably

at <u>Vista Print</u>. They will have everything you need. I created a stick-on window screen for the rear window of my truck with my company name and phone number on it and I have had people interested in my service call me from that window sign.

F. **Insurance:** Talk to your insurance rep and tell him that you need General Liability Insurance for your new business. It will cost you around $500 or so and you will need at least $500,000 coverage. You can't do business with any commercial accounts until you have it. As long as you don't have any employees, you probably won't need Workman's Comp insurance either, but keep in mind that if you do hire anyone, you have to assume that you WILL need it. I don't want the hassle of employees or the complications of such, but your income is limited to your own efforts and you have to consider this if you want your business to grow.

Step 3. Vendor Relationships

You can purchase your supplies and chemicals from the local hardware store, on-line retailer, pool supply store, or you can get a line of credit from a wholesaler. I pay one-half to one-third of retail because of my relationship with a wholesale supplier. There are three major ones in my area and I mostly stick with one.

If my call to them for supplies is in by 10am, they will be delivered to my doorstep by early afternoon the same day. I don't even have to be there. They leave a copy of the invoice and my business bank account gets debited automatically. You will have to do some of your own research to find out who your suppliers are in your area.

Step 4. Equipment

Pickup truck or van. I prefer a pickup truck because it is easier to access the chemicals from the bed of a pickup truck than from inside a van. Just keep a tight lid on your chemicals and you'll be alright. You also have to consider that you will be exposed to chemical odors all day long if you store your chemicals in a van or a vehicle where the passenger compartment is not separate from chemical storage. Luckily, chlorine is not considered a carcinogen but an irritant. It is highly corrosive and will eat its way through any material or metal it is exposed to. You don't want to be inhaling chlorine if you don't have to. Find a small size pickup that is preferably a 4 cylinder. I have an old 2000 Nissan with 175,000 miles on it and it still gets 21 mpg driving around all day long hauling heavy chemicals and equipment. I have a pool service friend that has a larger full-size pickup with an 8 cylinder and he gets, on a good day, 15mpg. Don't throw money away.

Pool Vacuum: There are several brands available, but the standard of the industry is **Hammerhead**. It will cost you on average $1,800 but will save you more time and effort than you can imagine. Don't fight it, buy one, and you won't regret it I guarantee it. It runs off of a marine deep cycle battery and basically uses a DC motor to vacuum al the debris, sand and dirt from the bottom of the pool. It uses a hitch attached to the back or your truck and large wheels to help it move it through high grass and such. You will get used to pulling that thing around to and from your truck hitch. Recharge the battery nightly and the battery will last you a year or more.

Adjustable poles: Use your supplier to recommend one. You may want more than one. Experience and your particular pools will determine that.

Nets: You will need a professional <u>leaf rake</u>. I recommend the PurityPool.com Red Baron. It will cost you twice as much as the Lowes/Home Depot type, but will last three times as long. You will also want the ultra-fine model as well that has the ability to catch the smallest of creatures and debris that you can't get with a larger mesh net.

Misc: Keep a portable tool kit with you at all times. You will probably also want to keep a large pipe wrench with you. The commercial plastic wrenches that are used to remove the pump strainer lids are just too lame sometimes and the pipe wrench works better. Even though the lid expressly says "Hand Tighten Only" on it, people still over tighten them and it ruins the rubber gasket. Buy yourself some silicone gasket ring lube from your supplier. The strainer housing won't seal properly without a new gasket and some good lube, but HAND TIGHTEN please. The pump vacuum will suck it down properly, so you don't need to overdo it. You will want some rags and a bucket. Get yourself a short hose with a pressure nozzle on it to clean filter elements with. The ones they sell to hook up an RV to a water supply are the best. <u>Rubber</u> <u>gloves</u> are a good thing sometimes. Buy a supply of <u>Magic Erasers</u> or the generic equivalent. It works really well for cleaning the upper tiles of pools.

Brushes: Wall brush. Get one that will last. Also you probably won't need one that is really big either because it won't work well in the corners. You will also need a <u>stainless steel</u> <u>wire brush</u> for stubborn algae and marks on the pool walls and bottom.

Step 5. Chemicals and Supplies

Chemicals are the heart and soul of your business and you need to understand what they do and how they work, and that is why attending a certification class is really necessary. I can only offer a brief explanation of what they are and how they are used. The rest is up to your discretion, knowledge and experience.

A. Chlorine and Bromine

Chlorine is primarily used in pools and Bromine is used primarily in spas, because it is more effective at high temperatures and is less irritating on the skin. These chemicals

are what kill the algae and pathogens in your

pool water and drinking water. The delivery

method of getting the chlorine in the water

to do its job can be different. The most

common method of pool professionals is

liquid chlorine filled up from your supplier in

yellow 2.5 gallon plastic jugs. Liquid chlorine

starts losing potency as soon as the factory

creates it, but it is widely used. You can also

get different forms of granular chlorine too,

and my personal favorites are the 3"

stabilized chlorine tablets. Chances are you

will use some combination of the above

mentioned. The generally accepted standard

is that a chlorine level of between 1 and 3 parts per million (ppm) is correct. I also know that in Florida in the summertime that if my pools were at a level of 1ppm for a day, they would be green the next day. I would never publicly recommend it, but you need to keep the chlorine level high in the summer in the south or you will be fighting algae all summer long.

B. Algaecides

There are many, but my favorites are "Tri-Chlor" for stubborn black algae and Sodium Bromide for all flavors of green, blue-green, and yellow algae. Keep a supply on-hand at all times. Sodium Bromide is also sold under the names of "Yellow Treat", "Swamp Treat" etc., but they are all basically Sodium Bromide. The so-called "Quats" also work well but are expensive and are sold specifically as algaecides. I like to use Copper Sulfate for long-term protection against algae as well. It goes into the water blueish, but dissipates and stays in the pool water for a good while. Don't over-do it though because it can stain the pool surface.

C. Stabilizer

Cyanuric acid is added to pools to keep the sun's ultraviolet rays from destroying all the expensive chlorine you've just added to your pool. It binds with the chlorine and acts as a sunscreen to the chlorine and slows down the degradation of available chlorine in the summer months in particular. Some people charge extra for a stabilizer treatment, but I don't. Stabilizer only needs to be added to pools once or twice a year.

D. Salt

Salt chlorination systems are becoming more and more popular and will represent a growing number of your pools and you need to keep a supply of pool salt with you at all times. I am not a fan of salt systems for reasons that I won't go into now. People need to understand that if they have a salt system, the way that their pool is sanitized is by the CHLORINE that is extracted from the salt by the salt cell. The salt does not sanitize the pool but the CHLORINE does. Thank you.

E. Ph Balancers

In order to maintain a consistent level of chlorine in the pool, the proper Ph must be maintained. Also, if the water is too acidic, it will corrode the pool finish and damage your equipment, and if it is too alkaline, you can get calcium build-up on the equipment and damage it as well. You also need to keep the Ph relatively neutral as well for human comfort on the skin.

You will use:

1. <u>Sodium Carbonate</u>. Also known as Ph+ to maintain the level of alkalinity.

2. <u>Sodium Bicarbonate</u>. Also known as baking soda. It is the easiest way to raise the Ph of the water (make it less acid) and is cheaper than Ph+.

3. <u>Hydrochloric Acid</u>. Also known as Muriatic acid. Sulfuric acid works too. When the water Ph is too high (alkaline), it needs to be brought down to a more neutral level by the addition of acid. When you use liquid chlorine you WILL need to add acid fairly often as liquid chlorine has a high Ph.

F. Chemical testing.

How do you know if you have the proper level of chemicals in the pool? You need to use a test kit. There are the liquid test kits and are not expensive, and there are the test strips. There are electronic testers but I don't use one because of the time and expense of using them. Time is everything in the pool business. The more pools you clean the more money you make. It is that simple. To that end, I recommend a bottle of 100 test strips. You walk up to your pool, dip a strip in the water and compare it to the chart on the bottle, and in 30 seconds you know the level

How to Start a Pool Service

of chlorine, Ph, hardness, stabilizer level, total alkalinity, and available chlorine. It is fast and efficient. It costs about 15 cents a strip but for all that it does in such a short time it is well worth it.

Step 6. How do I get customers?

Here is the easiest way and the way I got started. I purchased 17 existing accounts from someone who wanted to get out of the business. His heart wasn't in it and he wanted to go back to school to become a chef. I got his accounts and some basic equipment. He worked with me on each account for two weeks and then I was on my own. The 17 accounts were purchased indirectly through a pool route broker. There are many, and they specialize in pool accounts. It cost me $12,000 outright and I immediately began to make about $1,800 a month in revenue. He only had 17 accounts he acquired through a pool builder that he used to work for that didn't want to service the pools he built, so he would refer them to this guy. After three years he only had 17 accounts to sell. After I took over his accounts, through various methods of advertising and referrals, in six months I had 25 accounts, and in a year-and-a-half I had 56 accounts billing about $4,500 a month (about $55,000 yearly net with add-on business and repairs).

Here are the main methods to gain accounts:

1. Buy advertised routes for sale on Craigslist.org, or from a pool route broker.

2. Advertise in the local paper.

3. Referrals. Do good reliable work and people will recommend you to the people they know that may need your service.

4. Create a web site that people can find when they search on-line for pool services. Go to Craigslist to find someone to build one for you on the cheap.

5. Door hangers. Drop off a door hanger when you have time driving through

neighborhoods. You can see who has a pool

and who doesn't from the street.

6. Join a professional organization to get your

    name out like the Chamber of Commerce.

7. Set up a booth at your neighborhood fair and

    offer free water testing and coupons for the

    first month free for a six month contract.

8. Join Angie's List or Service Magic and pay for

    good quality leads.

To sum it all up--

If you don't mind hard work, the pool business

can be a great way to make a living. You will charge

anywhere from $60 to $110 a month to service a pool weekly. The profit margin is about 80% net of expenses, so if you are billing $5,000 a month gross, you will net approximately $4,000. Start-up costs are low and the profit margin is high. You will write off business expenses such as your phone, internet service, your truck and transportation/maintenance costs, and at least 25% of your home on your taxes. As long as you keep a steady clientele, you will never be unemployed. If you lose an account, and you will for various reasons, you replace it with another. Your income is based on many accounts and not just one.

Professionalism. You represent yourself. You are the company. Your appearance makes a difference. Cut your hair, shave, and wear decent clothes. Don't swear or smoke in front of your customers. Always be polite. And remember that no matter how wrong they are, the customer is always right. Just remember that this is a service business and the better you treat your customers, the more loyal they will be to you and the more referrals you will get. I tell my customers that I'm not trying to get rich, but just trying to make a living. Treat every pool as if it were your own.

Carpe Diem!

www.ingramcontent.com/pod-product-compliance
Lightning Source LLC
Chambersburg PA
CBHW072030190526
45166CB00015B/1684